The INTERNATIONAL SQUID COOKBOOK

The INTERNATIONAL SQUID COOKBOOK

By Isaac Cronin

Designed and illustrated by
Jeanne Jambu

ARIS BOOKS

Addison-Wesley Publishing Company, Inc.
Reading, Massachusetts   Menlo Park, California   New York
Don Mills, Ontario   Wokingham, England   Amsterdam   Bonn
Sydney   Singapore   Tokyo   Madrid   San Juan

Library of Congress Cataloging-in-Publication Data

Cronin, Isaac, 1948–
    The international squid cookbook.

    1. Cookery (Squid)   2. Cookery, Inter-
national.   I. Title.
TX748.S68C76   1988   641.6'94   88-35063
ISBN 0-201-19030-3

ISBN 0-201-19030-3
(Previously published by Harris Publishing Co., ISBN 0-943186-07-2)

We thank the following persons for permission to use their recipes. Any omissions or errors will be corrected in subsequent printings.

"Squid and leeks in red wine" from Richard Olney, *Simple French Food* (New York: Atheneum Publishers, 1974) Copyright © 1974 by Richard Olney. Reprinted with the permission of Atheneum Publishers.

"Calamares Rellenos con Jamon" from Alan Davidson, *Mediterranean Seafood* (London: Penguin Books, 1972) Copyright © 1972 by Alan Davidson. Reprinted with the permission of Alan Davidson.

Aris Books Editorial Office
and Test Kitchen
1621 Fifth St.
Berkeley, CA 94710

ABCDEFGHIJ-VB-898
First Addison-Wesley printing, December 1988

This book is dedicated to the millions of people around the world for whom squid is already a culinary delight, and to my son, Beau, who started eating squid when he was ten months old and can never seem to get enough, no matter how I cook it.

I would like to thank the following people for their support and for their contributions to this book: Ron Berger, Dixie Blake, Vince and Mary Bruno, Joyce Cole, Joan Eesley, Mike Flanagan, Pat Flanagan, Jeanne Jambu, Leonardo Oliveri, Terrel Seltzer, Gilbert Voss.

TABLE OF CONTENTS

In Praise of Squid

The first time I met the squid was on a cold, moonlight night on the Monterey Bay. Our fishing boat, The Three Sisters, caught twenty tons in its nets. I took a few pounds home and made myself a simple sauté. To my surprise, the squid were delicious. From that day I became a passionate lover of squid. Today, a growing number of people share my enthusiasm. We join the ranks of the hundreds of millions of people worldwide for whom squid is already a staple food. We have all discovered that squid is a delicious, inexpensive, nutritious and especially pure food which can be prepared as simply or as elaborately as one desires. And if you need still another reason to eat squid, here's one: It is ecologically sound. Squid is one of America's few underutilized acquatic species. California Fish and Game officials report that the squid supply is not being diminished by current levels of fishing; much of the catch is canned for export. Greater domestic demand would mean either more fresh and less canned squid, or increased fishing which the population permits. So enjoy your squid guiltlessly.

My own campaign to promote the culinary attributes of squid was conducted in relative obscurity, limited to writing an occasional magazine article, preparing squid dinners at home with friends, and making trips to various European and Asian restaurants which serve squid, until I met L. John Harris, the editor and publisher of this book. John is the author of *The Book of Garlic* and a champion of relatively unknown, healthy foods. He immediately recognized the value of squid which, not surprisingly, he called "the garlic of the sea."

As we began the initial preparations for this book, another sign of the squid's growing popularity reached us: America's first squid festival was presented to a large, enthusiastic audience in Santa Cruz, California on September 8, 1980.

I t is always nice to talk about people like the Santa Cruz clan who agree with my point of view, but in all honesty I must add that there are those who turn up their noses at the mere mention of squid, labelling it "bait." Well, two other delicious seafoods, herring and anchovies, are bait, too. I wonder if such culinary ostriches would have us avoid them along with snails, garlic and all other unusual and interesting foods which do not fit their narrow definition of acceptable fare.

I hope that this book will encourage food lovers to get more enjoyment from squid in as many ways as possible. *The International Squid Cookbook* has something for everyone: the step-by-step cleaning, stuffing and cooking instructions will help the initiate who has enjoyed squid in a restaurant but has never prepared it at home. The many recipes drawn from the great cuisines of the world will provide encouragement for the squid enthusiast looking for new pleasures. The chapters on the giant squid and squid fishing will inform the curious who want to discover the facts hidden behind the mystique of the squid. And then there are a few surprises. Read on to find them.

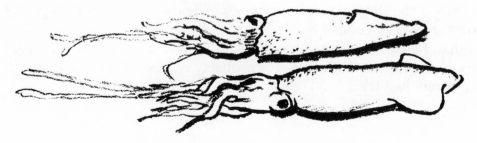

Portrait of the Squid

Squid is a mollusk, not a fish. It has firm flesh and contains very little natural juice. Contrary to some opinions, squid is not yukky.

The species of squid used in most of my recipes, and the one most commonly eaten in the United States, is the Monterey squid (*loligo opalescens*). It does not have tough muscle fibers and there is no need to tenderize it. In fact, pounding the Monterey squid may only turn it into an inedible pulp. A squid eaten on the East coast and in England, *loligo pealei*, is very similar to Monterey squid.

An increasingly popular variety, likely to rival Monterey squid in the coming years, is the larger Grande Calamari caught in the waters of the Gulf of California off Mexico and imported to the United States already filleted. Straight out of the water the large squid have tougher flesh and they are tenderized by machine before being packed and frozen. Use Grande Calamari interchangably with Monterey squid except for recipes calling for a loose stuffing. Hard stuffings, such as cheese, will work fine with Grande Calamari.

When heated, squid protein becomes firm rapidly and then turns chewy until long cooking breaks down the muscle. Much of the squid's reputation as a tough food comes from lack of knowledge of this simple fact. Sautés should be cooked no longer than three minutes and stews no less than twenty minutes. Squid cooked for less than twenty minutes or more than about three minutes probably will be tough. If you don't believe me, just try it.

Squid absorbs water quickly from marinades and sauces. Thus it can be prepared rapidly and still acquire all the flavoring of its accompaniments. Marinades *do* help the flavor of squid, but only up to a point. Squid should never be marinated too long. Half an hour is probably the optimum time. After that, the meat starts to soften and may even take on a bitter taste if lemon or vinegar is used.

Squid, like any seafood, is fragile. It should be refrigerated until just before use to keep it as fresh as possible.

The dark ink of the squid is its means of defense. It shoots it at intruders who venture too close, creating an obscuring cloud behind which the squid makes a quick getaway. The ink itself is a salty, black liquid which makes an excellent flavoring for sauces. It is, not suprisingly, water soluble. Don't worry if you get ink on your hands or clothes. It washes right out.

A mong those who understand and appreciate it, the squid has earned the affectionate title of "the poor man's abalone"—and with good reason. Both are mollusks—the squid's shell is its plastic backbone which has become an internal structure; both have firm, mildly sweet meat. The squid is, if anything, more versatile. The smaller varieties don't require tenderizing, and the body can be stuffed with a variety of ingredients. There is even a recipe for squid abalone-style (page 31). The end result tastes remarkably like abalone.

Varieties of Edible Squid Commonly Found in Europe and America

1. *Loligo pealei,* also called the Atlantic long-finned squid, is approximately 12 inches long, with a slender body and short tentacles. It is caught in the Eastern coastal waters of North America.

2. *Loligo vulgaris* is similar in looks and length to *Loligo pealei.* It is found in the North Sea and the Mediterranean Sea along North Africa.

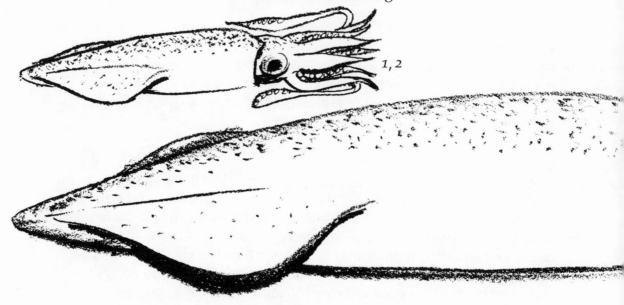

3. *Dosidicus gigas,* also called the giant squid or Grande Calamari, reaches about 5 feet in length. Gracefully proportioned, with long tapering tentacles, it is found along the Pacific coast of South America up to the Mexican-U.S. border.

4. *Loligo opalescens*, also called the common Pacific or Monterey squid, is approximately 8 inches long, with a slender body, short fins, and short, thick tentacles. It is caught in the Western coastal waters of North America.

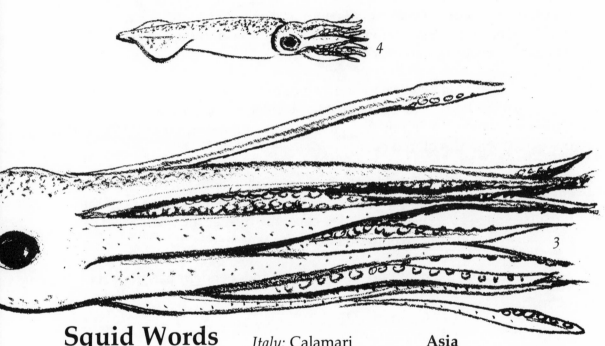

Squid Words

Europe

Denmark: Blaeksprutter
France: Encornet
Germany: Kalmar
Greece: Kalamarakia
Holland: Pijlinktvis

Italy: Calamari
Norway: Blekkspruter
Poland: Kalmar
Portugal: Lula
Russia: Kal'mar
Spain: Calamar
Sweden: Kalmar

Asia

China: Yao
Indonesia: Tjume
Japan: Ika
The Philippines: Pusit
Thailand: Pla Muek
Vietnam: Mục

BUYING SQUID

Fresh Squid

1. Fresh squid—squid that has been caught 24-36 hours prior to purchase, is distinguishable by its odor and color. The flesh exudes a mildly sweet smell. Any other aroma, fishy or acrid, indicates the squid has been out of the water for several days.

2. The skin should be close to an ivory color beneath the dark spots which dot the body. The spots themselves tend to increase in number with age. Any yellowing of the skin is a sure sign the squid is old. Never buy squid with discolored flesh.

3. One sure way to test for age, which is possible only after buying a batch, is the ease with which the transparent quill comes loose from the flesh (see page 20). The easier it detaches, the fresher the squid. You can generally rely on your fish market to advise you.

4. You are more likely to find fresh squid at independent fish markets.

Frozen Squid

1. Squid freezes well since it has no blood, the decomposition of which affects flavor.

2. In many areas of the United States it is only available frozen, usually in 5-pound and 3-pound boxes packed in Monterey or San Pedro. These boxes are available in many areas where you wouldn't expect to find squid, like Dallas.

3. The block of squid can be defrosted by complete immersion in cold water. A 5-pound box will thaw in one hour or less.

4. Grande Calamari fillets are only sold frozen, since they are imported from Mexico. They are generally packed in 5-pound boxes, and are marketed in a variety of cuts.

5. If you are able to buy large quantities of fresh Monterey Squid and would like to freeze them, you can clean the squid first. Clean (see page 18) and wash the squid and drain well in a colander. Shake off excess moisture. Put them in a double plastic bag and close securely. Squid will keep for 2 months in the freezer section of a refrigerator, according to Pat Flanagan of General Fish, one of the largest American distributors of squid. But Flanagan recommends that squid and other seafood be kept in a separate freezer if possible. Frost-free refrigerators draw the moisture out of food, decreasing flavor, while frequent use results in uneven freezing. The temperature is raised each time the door is opened. In a separate freezer which is opened not more than once or twice a day, squid will keep up to 6 months.

RAW MATERIALS

Squid Nutrition

A 6-ounce serving—the quantity obtained by allowing 3 pounds of uncleaned Monterey squid for 4 people—yields:

114 grams of water
30 grams of protein
2.5 grams of fat
2.9 grams of carbohydrate
153 calories
(100 calories for 6 oz of Grande Calamari fillets)

To obtain the equivalent amount of protein from tofu (bean curd), one of the healthiest and most economical sources of protein available, one would consume 2½ times as many calories.

Ink as Ink as Medicine

If this book had been published five hundred yars ago, it very well might have been printed with the ink from the squid or cuttlefish. Sepia, the dark liquid from these two cephalopods, was the source of a good deal of Europe's ink until other dyes were invented. When it is diluted, the ink turns a dark brown, thus the origin of the technique of sepiatoning. Today, sepia is still used for pen and ink drawings because, although it is relatively expensive, sepia can be diluted almost indefinitely, allowing for great variations in shading.

Ink straight from the squid has no known medicinal use, but for the science of homeopathy, sepia is an important substance.

A Word About Tentacles

The tentacles of the squid are edible. In fact, they are delicious. They constitute a substantial portion of the squid's edible flesh, and you should use them unless some

hangup makes it impossible to do so. And even then, you should try them before you pass judgment.

I do not refer to the tentacles in the individual recipes, because I assume you will use them. In all stuffing recipes they can be braised or baked whole, along with the bodies. In salads, barbecues, sautés and stir-frys they should be included with the squid rings or pieces either whole or chopped. The one dish which tentacles seem to detract from rather than enhance is Baked Squid (page 32), and then only because a certain texture is being sought. The taste of the dish would in no way be altered by including the tentacles.

A Cleaner Way to Clean Squid

Many people have told me they would eat more squid if it were not so unpleasant to clean it. The method presented here eliminates many potentially unpleasant aspects of squid cleaning. You needn't touch the entrails with your fingers, nor labor over each squid.

In using our method, the edible skin is removed.

In any case, precleaned squid is becoming increasingly available as are the Grande Calamari fillets.

CLEANING INSTRUCTIONS

Squid Anatomy

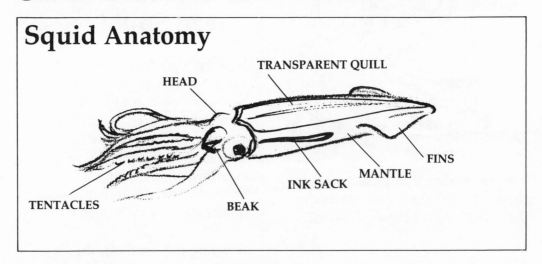

TRANSPARENT QUILL

HEAD

TENTACLES

BEAK

INK SACK

MANTLE

FINS

1. Cut off the tentacles just above the eye. Save them.

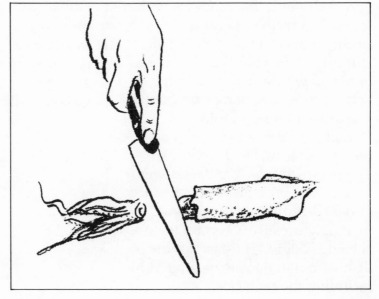

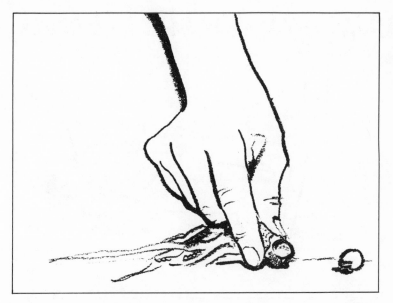

2. Squeeze out the beak, the squid's mouth, which looks like a garbanzo bean. Discard it.

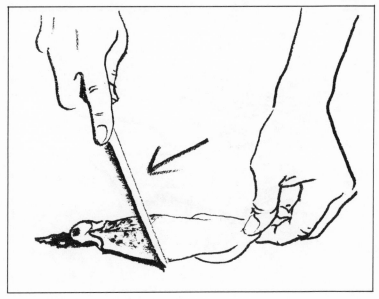

3. Hold the blade of a large knife almost flat against the body of the squid and scrape from the tail to the open end of the body cavity. (If you cut through the skin, move the blade closer to parallel with the body.)

4. Turn the squid over and repeat this procedure. By now all of the entrails should be squeezed out. Dispose of them. If you can feel any remaining entrails in the squid body, remove by hand or spoon.

5. Stab the transparent quill which protrudes from the body with a knife and hold it fast. Pull the body away. The quill should remain under the knife. Discard the quill. Once you have completed this basic procedure there are 3 options:

Whole
You can leave the body whole for stuffing.

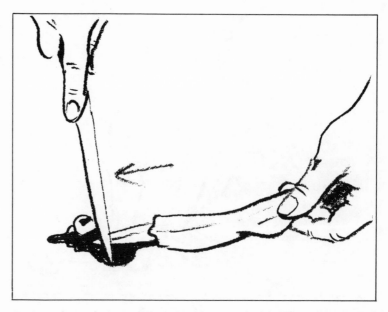

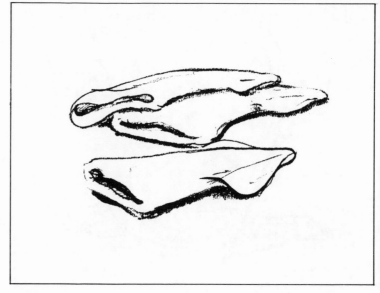

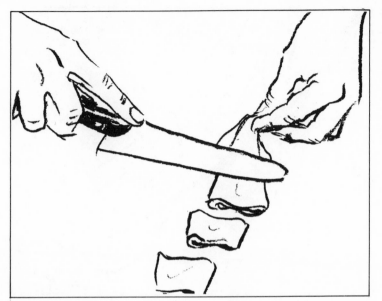

Rings

Cut across the body to make rings. One inch is a good size. You may cut them smaller if you like.

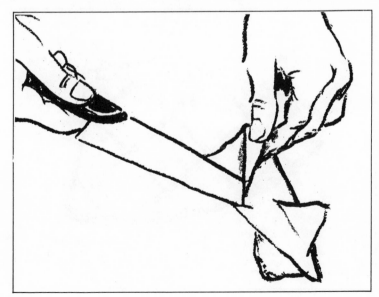

Fillets

To prepare squid for Chinese stir-fry or for abalone-style dishes, make a cut along the entire length of the body through one layer of the skin. Pull off the two fins. The skin will come with it. Flatten the body. The squid steaks or fillets are now ready to be breaded.

Chinese Style

The Chinese crosshatch the fillets to allow more of the surface to be exposed to the heat. In addition, it makes for a more attractive dish. Make shallow cuts diagonally across the body spaced ¾ inch apart. Don't pierce through the skin.

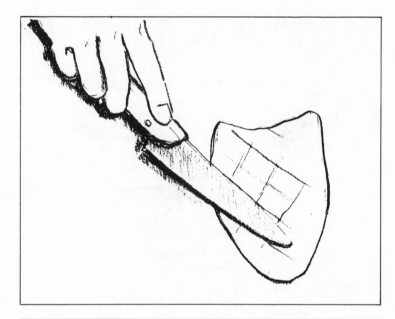

Repeat in the other direction, cutting at an oblique angle to the first cuts. Continue down the body. This technique takes a little practice, and the result is worth it.
T.) FRENCH

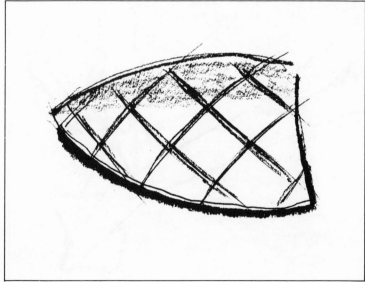

STUFFING A SQUID

The body of the California squid is about 1½ inches in diameter, which makes it somewhat difficult to fill. Fortunately, a simple baker's tool—a pastry bag and large attachment (¾ inch or bigger)—works wonderfully for a number of the stuffing mixtures, especially those with a moist consistency.

Ground meat works well in the pastry bag, as does crab in white sauce (page 36). Dryer stuffings like those with rice do not pass easily through the tip. It is best to spoon them in, even though it takes a little longer. Recipes calling for ingredients such as cheese or ham chunks, as in Squid San Jose (page 29) and Squid Stuffed with Smoked Ham (page 54), are easy when you use your hands. Fill the squid ¾ full or less. The bodies shrink as they cook and may burst if they are too packed.

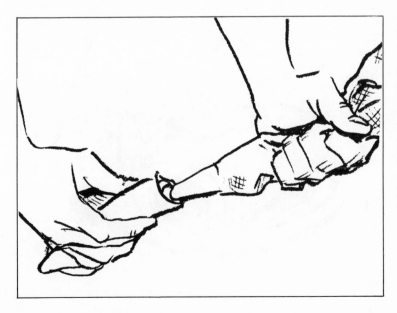

The Pastry Bag Technique

Fill a pastry bag with a soft homogeneous stuffing. Put the metal tip inside the squid's body. Squeeze down the bag until the squid is ¾ full. Seal the end by running a toothpick in and out through the skin close to the open end.

The Finger Technique

Larger, firm ingredients like ham, cheese, and chiles are simply placed inside the body with the fingers. Seal with a toothpick as in the pastry bag technique.

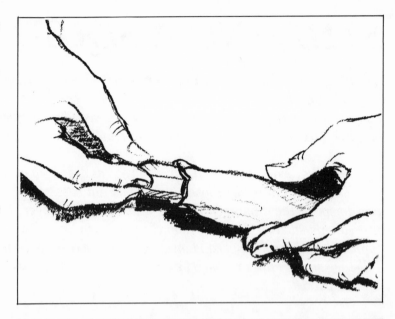

The Spoon Technique

Firm, finely chopped mixtures are spooned into the body. With one hand lift up the open end, with the other fill a teaspoon and push it into the body. Repeat as many times as necessary. Seal with a toothpick.

The Grande Calamari Technique

Stuffing the Grande Calamari is like stuffing a piece of flank steak. Place the solid ingredients on top of the steak. Roll it up slowly. Secure with several toothpicks or with string tied in at least two places.

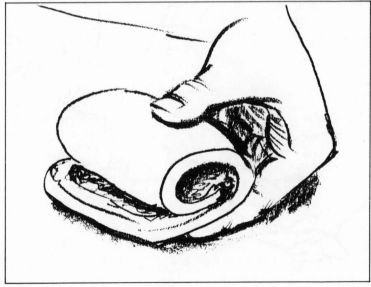

WAYS TO COOK SQUID

1. **Stir-fry:** The most common method for preparing squid in Thailand and China. After the oil, herbs, spices and sauce are prepared, the squid is added to the wok or frying pan, accompanied by vigorous stirring. Over high heat, the squid is cooked for 2 to 3 minutes. The sweet flavor and firm texture are preserved.

2. **Sauté:** The Western equivalent of stir-fry, sautéeing is a slightly slower cooking process.

3. **Grilling:** Squid are wonderful grilled over charcoal. Cook them only a few minutes on each side, then dip them in a sauce or eat them with lemon.

4. **Deep-frying:** This method is employed all over the world and is probably the most common mode of preparation. A dry or wet coating may be used. The squid pieces are done as soon as the coating browns.

5. **Braising:** Braising or stewing is slow cooking in liquid. The squid loses its characteristic firmness, but is tender and full of flavor absorbed from the liquid. Usually, braising requires a minimum of 20 minutes.

6. **Baking:** Many American-style recipes which approach squid as though it were abalone require baking. The squid is cut open, coated, and then baked for at least 20 minutes. Baking is also a way to cook stuffed squid.

7. **Pan braising:** Squid which are filled with precooked stuffing may be cooked in a little liquid in a frying pan.

8. No cooking: Squid is eaten raw with sushi rice.

9. Blanching: For many salads, squid is prepared by immersing the rings in boiling water for 30 seconds.

10. Steaming: The Japanese steam stuffed squid and then add them to soups and stews.

INTRODUCTION TO RECIPES

1. *All the recipes in this book, unless otherwise indicated, are for 4 people.*

2. *Recipe quantities for squid refer to whole, uncleaned Monterey squid unless the Grande Calamari fillets are specified. To substitute Grande Calamari fillets for Monterey squid rings and pieces, thaw the fillets for 30 minutes, then cut them into ½-inch strips or 1-inch squares and use as you would Monterey squid.*

3. *The methods of cleaning squid are described on page 18. They are not explained with each recipe.*

4. *Each recipe is presented according to its most frequent use. Some recipes included as salads or appetizers could become main courses by increasing the quantities of all the ingredients, and vice versa.*

5. *Fresh and frozen squid may be used interchangeably in all the recipes. Squid fillets can be used in all recipes except some which require stuffing.*

6. *The recipes list all the ingredients and describe all the techniques necessary to complete the dish. Almost all the recipes can be made from ingredients available at the supermarket. A few of the Asian dishes require ingredients more difficult to obtain. Even these can usually be purchased at an Asian grocery or gourmet store.*

7. *The use of salt, pepper and garlic is a very individual matter. Salt and pepper are simply listed without quantities. For garlic, a range of possible amounts, from light to garlicky, is usually given.*

8. *When appropriate, I have included serving suggestions and suitable beverages.*

9. *Olive oil is the favored oil in all of the Mediterranean recipes. Asians traditionally cook with a tasteless oil such as peanut oil or safflower oil. For the rest of the recipes, the choice of oil is up to the cook.*

AMERICAN RECIPES

Squid San Jose
Squid á la Abalonetti
California Grande Calamari
Squid Sautéed Abalone Style
Baked Squid
Squid Filé Gumbo
Fish Stock
*Squid Steak á la Anthony's
    Fish Grotto*
Squid Parmigiana
*Squid Pasta Sauce with
    White Wine*
*Squid Stuffed with Crab in
    Mornay Sauce*
Squid Sauté

Squid San Jose

This recipe was given to me by a friend from San Jose, California—thus its name. It has a Mexican flavor, though I have never been able to locate such a recipe in any Mexican cookbook. This is a good dish to serve to people who aren't sure if they like squid. I have won over many people to the cause with Squid San Jose.

3 lbs squid, cleaned and left whole
½ lb mild cheese (Jack is best)
1 large can whole mild green chiles
1 cup canned tomatoes, cut in
**   half and drained**
Juice of 2 lemons
Salt and pepper to taste

Preheat oven to 350°

Slice chiles lengthwise into pieces 2 to 3 inches long and ¼ inch wide. Cut cheese into finger-sized pieces. Stuff squid with one piece each of Jack cheese and green chile. Seal each with a toothpick. Layer squid in a baking dish. Sprinkle with salt and pepper, cover with tomatoes and lemon juice, and bake for 20 minutes.

I serve this dish with beer. It seems to enhance its Mexican flavor.

Squid á la Abalonetti

Abalonetti's on Fisherman's Wharf in Monterey opened fourteen years ago as a restaurant devoted primarily to the popularization of squid. In the ensuing years they have served over a hundred tons of squid prepared according to six different recipes. Here's their classic.

2 lbs squid, cleaned and cut open
  into flat pieces
½ cup evaporated milk
1 egg, beaten
1 tsp salt
⅛ tsp pepper
1 cup cracker meal
Oil

Combine milk, egg, salt and pepper.

Dip squid in mixture and roll in cracker meal. Place squid in a single layer in hot oil in a 10-inch frying pan. Fry at a moderate heat until lightly browned. Turn carefully. Cook the other side. Drain on absorbent paper. Serve with lemon wedges.

California Grande Calamari

This recipe comes from Ocean Garden Products, a San Diego based company with a strong belief in the future of the Grande Calamari. It serves 4.

4 Grande Calamari fillets
½ lb Monterey jack cheese
4 oz can mild green chiles
4 oz can sweet red chiles
1 egg, beaten
2 cups breading
Oil for deep frying

Lay strips of Monterey jack cheese, green chiles and red chiles in the center of each Grande Calamari fillet. Roll steak into a tube shape and secure with toothpicks or string.

Dip into egg, then roll in the breading. Heat oil to 350°. Deep-fry until golden brown, about 4 minutes. Pat off excess oil and serve hot.

Squid Sautéed Abalone Style

3 lbs squid, cleaned and cut open into flat pieces

2 cups breadcrumbs

4 oz each, grated romano and parmesan cheeses

1 egg

½ cup milk

Butter or vegetable oil

Lemon wedges

Salt and pepper to taste

Combine breadcrumbs and cheeses in a paper bag. Mix egg and milk in a small bowl. Dip each squid into the liquid and coat thoroughly. Put into bag and shake vigorously. Repeat for each squid.

Heat 6 Tbs or more of butter or oil in a large, heavy frying pan over high heat. Add to pan as many squid as will fit in one layer. Fry until browned and then turn over. Brown on the other side, then remove from the pan. Serve immediately. Repeat the process for the next batch or, if you like, use 2 skillets simultaneously.

Garnish with chopped parsley and serve with lemon wedges.

Baked Squid

This is a rich dish, reminiscent of lasagne. The squid acquires a pasta-like consistency during baking. This is one recipe for which tentacles detract from the consistency of the dish.

3 lbs squid, cleaned and filleted
  (see page 21)

2 cups breadcrumbs

1 cup milk

1 egg

½ lb provolone cheese,
   thinly sliced

2 oz parmesan cheese, grated

Salt and pepper to taste

Preheat oven to 400°

Mix breadcrumbs and grated parmesan together. Beat the egg. Add it to milk in a medium-sized bowl. Coat each piece of squid with the egg-milk mixture. Immediately cover it with breadcrumbs. The easiest way to do this is to put breadcrumbs in a bag. Add squid and shake vigorously.

In a baking dish, alternately layer squid and slices of provolone cheese. The top layer should be cheese. Sprinkle with salt and pepper. Bake until breadcrumbs brown, about 20 minutes.

Serve hot with a dry white wine.

Squid Filé Gumbo

Gumbo is a Louisiana classic; good especially for those who like their food hot.

2 cups Fish Stock

3 lbs squid, cleaned and cut into rings

2 scallions, chopped

2 stalks celery, chopped

2 bell peppers, chopped

1 cup canned tomatoes with juice

2-10 cloves garlic, minced

3 bay leaves

1 tsp filé powder

Salt and pepper to taste

Cayenne to taste

1-4 Tbs vegetable oil

Sauté garlic in oil in a large, heavy casserole or stock pot over low heat until lightly browned. Add stock, tomatoes, scallions, celery, bell pepper, bay leaves, salt and pepper. Simmer, covered, for 15 minutes.

Add squid, turn up heat to a medium boil and cook 3 minutes longer. Turn down heat to below boiling and add filé powder. Stir, heat 30 seconds more, remove from the flame. Sprinkle with cayenne.

Serve in bowls over rice with beer and toasted French bread or baguettes.

Fish Stock

3 quarts water

2 lbs fish heads and/or collars

2 carrots, roughly chopped

2 onions, roughly chopped

4 cloves peeled garlic, whole

3 bay leaves

½ cup parsley, whole stems

Simmer all the ingredients in a covered pot for 45 minutes. Skim off the foam every 10 minutes. Strain through a sieve or through cheesecloth.   Salt and pepper to taste.

Fish stock may be frozen for up to 1 month, or refrigerated for 3 or 4 days.

Squid Steak á la Anthony's Fish Grotto

The large Mexican squid were introduced into America in 1975. A temperature inversion off San Diego allowed the warmer waters from Mexico to drift north bringing with them Grande Calamari. They began turning up in the nets of American fishermen who were unfamiliar with the Monterey squid's larger cousin. As they have often done when they catch an unusual species, the area's fishermen brought their catch to Tod Ghio of Anthony's Fish Grotto. Tod is a restaurateur and fish market operator known for his willingness to experiment with unusual varieties of seafood. He took some of the squid to his restaurant, cooked it and served the steaks to his patrons. It was, so they tell me, "tough as hell." But Tod didn't give up. He cut away 4 layers of skin and uncovered a fillet which, with a little tenderizing, proved to be delicious. Today Tod's restaurants and many others serve Grande Calamari fillets.

1 lb Grande Calamari fillets
1 egg
1 tsp water
2 cups breadcrumbs made from French bread
½ tsp dried parsley
½ tsp oregano
½ tsp thyme
1 Tb butter
1 Tb olive oil
1 Tb vegetable oil

Mix egg and water in a bowl. Combine bread crumbs and herbs. Dip each fillet in the egg and then coat with bread crumbs.

Fry fillets in a large, heavy frying pan in oil, olive oil and butter over medium heat. When the fillets have browned, turn them over and brown the other side. Serve with lemon-garlic butter (see page 40).

Squid Parmigiana

**1 recipe of Squid Steak á la
  Anthony**
1 cup tomato sauce
**¼ lb provolone or romano cheese,
  thinly sliced**

After the fillets are browned, place
them in a baking dish and coat
with your favorite tomato sauce.
Top with slices of cheese. Broil
under high heat until the cheese
melts. Serve immediately.

Squid Pasta Sauce with White Wine

*This is a pasta sauce for those who like
their squid straight, with plenty of
garlic.*

**3 lbs squid, cleaned and cut into
  rings**
½ cup dry white wine
½ cup chicken stock
4-8 cloves garlic, minced
2 Tbs parsley, chopped
2-3 Tbs vegetable oil

Sauté garlic in oil in a large, heavy
frying pan over low heat until
lightly browned. Add white wine,
stock and parsley. Simmer until
sauce is reduced by ⅓. Turn up
heat to a moderate boil. Add squid
and cook for 3 minutes.

Serve over spinach fettucine or
other thick pasta.

Squid Stuffed with Crab in Mornay Sauce

This is a rich and elegant dish which tastes a little like canneloni; 2 pounds of squid is enough for 4.

2 lbs squid, cleaned and left whole
½ lb crabmeat, fresh, frozen or canned
1 cup milk
1 Tb butter
1½ Tbs flour
2 oz romano cheese, grated
2 oz gruyere cheese, grated
Salt and pepper to taste

Heat oven to 350°.

In a small, heavy saucepan melt butter over low heat. Meanwhile, slowly heat milk to a boil in another pan. Gradually add flour to butter, whisking as you pour. Continue to cook over low heat for 2 minutes. Try not to brown the *roux* (the flour-butter mixture). Remove from heat and add milk all at once. Whisk vigorously and then return to heat. Boil slowly for 1 minute, then add cheeses, salt and pepper. Crab is salty, so watch out. Cook for 30 seconds more, whisking all the while. Remove from heat and after a few minutes pour half the white sauce into a bowl and combine with crab. Allow to cool slightly.

Stuff each squid with crab and sauce mixture using a pastry sack (see page 23) and seal with a toothpick.

Layer the squid in a baking dish and cover with remaining white sauce. Bake for 15 minutes. Turn up heat to broil and put dish under the flame until top layer turns light brown.

Squid stuffed with crab is excellent served with a dry white wine. Follow with a green salad tossed with a vinaigrette dressing.

Squid Sauté

The easiest and, many people think, the best way to prepare squid is to sauté it. The basic recipe and variations provided here do not begin to cover the many ways to sauté squid. This dish takes 10 minutes or less to make once you have cleaned the squid.

**3 lbs squid, cleaned and cut into
rings
2 Tbs parsley, chopped
4 Tbs butter or olive oil
4 cloves garlic, minced (optional)
Lemon wedges
Salt and pepper to taste**

If you are using garlic, sauté it in 1 Tb of olive oil or butter in a heavy frying pan over low heat until it is lightly browned. Turn up to a medium-high flame. Add the rest of the oil, and when it is hot the squid, parsley, salt and pepper. Sauté for 3 minutes.

Serve with lemon wedges and boiled or fried potatoes.

Variations:

1. Add quartered, cooked artichoke hearts or coarsely sliced beets along with the squid.
2. Substitute 1 tsp of dried or fresh dill, or 2 Tbs of fresh basil for parsley.
3. Substitute 1 tsp cayenne for black pepper.

EUROPEAN RECIPES

MEDITERRANEAN AREA

Deep-Fried Squid
Dipping Sauces
   Tamarind-Raisin Chutney
   Lemon- Garlic Butter
   Roughly-Chopped Garlic
   Aioli — Mayonnaise
Squid Vinaigrette

GREECE

Squid Stuffed Greek Style
Barbecued Squid

FRANCE

Squid Stuffed with Spinach and
   Seafood
Squid Biscayan
Squid Marseillaise
Squid and Leeks in Red Wine
Squid Tomato Pasta Sauce

ITALY

Mary Bruno's Squid Balls
Squid Cacciuco

PORTUGAL

Lulas Rechadas

SPAIN

Calamares en su Tinta
Calamares Rellenos con Jamón

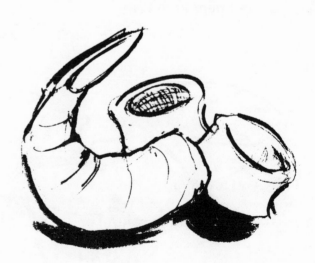

Deep-Fried Squid

Deep-fried squid is one of the most popular seafood dishes in the world. It is made in almost every country where squid is eaten. Once you taste it, you'll see why. The rings emerge juicy, sweet and crisp. Served with several dipping sauces, this dish makes an excellent hors d'oeuvre or main course. This recipe calls for a dry coating. Wet coatings, such as tempura batter, are delicious, too, though they are a little more trouble to apply.

3 lbs squid, cleaned and cut into rings
Flour for coating, at least 3 cups
Salt and pepper to taste
Oil for deep frying. Peanut oil is best.

Dry the rings thoroughly with paper towels. Coat with flour, to which salt and pepper have been added.

Heat oil to 350° in a deep-fat fryer or heavy casserole. If you don't have a temperature control or thermometer, you can guess at the temperature by dropping a few drops of water into the oil. It should sizzle immediately on contact. Plunge basket laden with one layer of squid into oil which should bubble vigorously on contact. If you don't have a basket for deep-frying, use a large spoon or tongs to immerse squid in oil, and to remove. Fry until coating turns golden brown, about 3 or 4 minutes.

Remove squid and drain. Turn down heat to moderate until just before you are ready to cook the next batch; oil will overheat when the fryer is empty. Remove excess oil from squid with paper towels.

Serve rings hot with any of the dipping sauces described below or with lemon wedges. Cole slaw is a natural with deep-fried squid.

Dipping Sauces

TAMARIND-RAISIN CHUTNEY

1 cup currants or raisins
4-6 tsps tamarind concentrate (available at gourmet stores, Indian and Middle Eastern groceries)
1 Tb ginger, minced
1 tsp fresh green chile pepper, minced, or substitute cayenne

Purée all the ingredients in a food processor or blender. Adjust tartness and spicyness to taste.

LEMON-GARLIC BUTTER

Juice of 2 lemons
4 Tbs butter
1-6 cloves garlic, minced

Fry garlic in 1 Tb of butter until lightly browned. Add rest of butter and lemon. When butter melts, sauce is ready.

ROUGHLY-CHOPPED GARLIC

Actually, this is not a sauce, but it was such a hit at one squid party that I am including it here.

Throw in a handful of chopped garlic 1 minute before the squid rings are ready to come out. Remove golden brown garlic with a mesh scoop after you take out the squid. Be sure you get all the pieces out. Anything left in the oil will burn and impart a bitter flavor to the next batch of squid.

AIOLI — MAYONNAISE

This French garlic mayonnaise recipe is from The Book of Garlic. *It makes a great dipping sauce for squid. You can make it in a blender for speed, but it tastes better made the authentic way.*

4 cloves garlic
2-3 raw egg yolks
Salt and pepper to taste
2 cups olive oil
2 Tb lemon juice or vinegar
1-2 Tb water or additional
    lemon juice
½ tsp Dijon mustard (optional)

Peel the garlic and pound in a mortar until smooth. Add the egg yolks and seasoning. Continue pounding until the paste is smooth. Then beat in lemon juice with a whisk. Start adding the oil a drop at a time while continuing to whisk. If you use a blender, whirl the garlic, lemon juice and egg yolks for about a minute until smooth and then add a slow, thin stream of oil while blender is still on high. Do not over liquify! The sauce should be thick like mayonnaise. If the sauce gets too thick, add water or lemon juice. Makes about 3 cups.

Squid Vinaigrette

Squid is great in salads. It can be combined with other cold seafood and a vinaigrette dressing, or included with other vegetables such as beets, potatoes and tomatoes to accent a green salad. This recipe calls for artichoke hearts. Mushrooms would be just as delicious.

1½ lbs squid, cleaned and cut into rings
6 Tbs olive oil
2 Tbs wine vinegar
1 Tb lemon juice
1 8-oz can artichoke hearts
1 Tb parsley, chopped
Romaine lettuce
Salt and pepper to taste

Combine oil, vinegar, lemon, salt and pepper in a large bowl. Add artichoke hearts. Marinate for at least 2 hours.

Immerse squid rings in boiling water for 30 seconds. Drain and cool. Add squid and parsley to vinaigrette. Marinate for 30 minutes.

Serve over a bed of lettuce.

Squid Stuffed Greek Style

This is the classic Greek stuffing recipe. The filling is similar to that used for stuffed tomatoes and bell peppers. This dish is excellent served warm or cold, as well as hot.

3 lbs squid, cleaned and left whole
2 cups cooked rice (brown or white)
2 Tbs parsley, chopped
2 Tbs fresh mint, chopped
4 Tbs raisins
2 Tbs pine nuts
1 cup canned tomatoes, cut in half
Salt and pepper to taste

Preheat oven to 350°.

In a bowl combine rice, parsley, mint, raisins and pine nuts. Stuff the squid using a small spoon. Seal each with a toothpick. Layer squid in a baking dish. Cover with tomatoes. Bake for 20 minutes.

Serve at any temperature, but do not reheat.

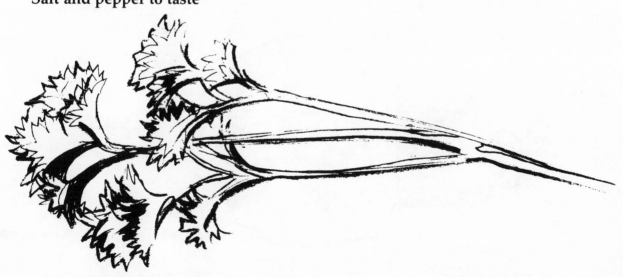

Barbecued Squid

This recipe sounds too easy to be true. It isn't. As with any grilled seafood, the fresher the ingredients and the simpler the cooking, the better the end result. Barbecued squid and an anise-flavored aperitif like pernod, ricard, ouzo or raki, make a wonderful combination.

3 lbs squid, cleaned and cut into rings
Lemon-garlic butter (see page 40)

Make a fire, preferably with firewood or Mexican charcoal, started from paper and kindling. Skewer the squid. When coals are red hot, barbecue the rings for 2-3 minutes a side, or until they are brown. Some recipes for grilled squid suggest marinating them. I omit this procedure because it adds flavor at the expense of softening the flesh.

Serve hot with lemon-garlic butter.

NOTE: Commercial charcoal and lighter fluid are petroleum products. They impart an oily flavor to food. Hardwood, or Mexican charcoal, a commercial product, which is made by burning down mesquite, both give a nice flavor and are certainly less toxic than petrochemicals. Mexican charcoal is available in Northern California through Lazzari Fuel Company, San Francisco.

Squid Stuffed with Spinach and Seafood

Spinach is a wonderful companion for squid. Its own mild flavor enhances and complements the mild taste of squid. After the dish is cooked and the body becomes slightly transparent, the dark green of the spinach is beautiful under the skin.

3 lbs squid, cleaned and left whole
1 large bunch fresh spinach
  chopped, or one box frozen
  spinach
24 mussels or large clams, or one
  large can whole clams, drained
4 cloves garlic, chopped (optional)
½ cup dry white wine

Preheat oven to 350°.

If you are using fresh mollusks, scrub their shells under cold running water. Steam over boiling water until they open. Cool and remove the meat.

Cook the spinach. Combine spinach and mussels or clams.

Sauté optional garlic over low heat in a frying pan until lightly browned. Add this to spinach-seafood mixture. Fill each squid with the stuffing and seal with a toothpick. Layer squid in a baking dish, add the wine, and bake for 20 minutes.

Serve hot with a dry white wine.

Variation:
Abalone or scallops cooked and chopped into medium-size pieces can be substituted for the clams.

Squid Biscayan

This Basque dish has an unusual touch. The squid is flambéed in brandy, and then quickly sautéed. Definitely a recipe for the confirmed squid lover looking for a new thrill.

3 lbs squid, cleaned and cut into rings
2 shallots, finely chopped
2 onions, finely chopped
2 green bell peppers, chopped
1 large can tomatoes, chopped
4 or more cloves garlic, minced
1 Tb parsley, chopped
3 oz brandy
1 tsp paprika
¼ cup olive oil
Salt and pepper to taste

In a large, heavy frying pan sauté onions, garlic, shallots, and bell pepper in 6 Tbs of olive oil over low heat. When onions are transparent, remove vegetables from pan and set aside.

Return pan to high heat and add remaining 2 Tbs of olive oil. When it is hot, add the squid. Cook for 1 minute, and then coat with brandy. Heat brandy and ignite. Turn down flame and toss the pan slightly; when the alcohol has burned off, the flame will subside. Add the sautéed vegetables, tomatoes, parsley, paprika, and salt and pepper. Sauté slowly for 4 minutes.

Serve immediately over rice with a strong, dry red wine.

Variation:

Shrimp makes a nice addition to this dish. Substitute ½ pound of raw, shelled shrimp for 1 pound of squid.

Squid Marseillaise

3 lbs squid, cleaned and left whole
Squid tentacles
½ cup breadcrumbs made from
   French bread or a baguette
2 Tbs parsley, finely chopped
4 cloves garlic, chopped
1 cup canned tomatoes,
   drained and chopped
1 onion, finely chopped
½ cup white wine
½ cup water
5 Tbs olive oil

Chop tentacles into small pieces.

In a frying pan sauté garlic over low heat in 2 Tbs of olive oil until lightly browned. Turn up to a medium flame and add tomatoes, parsley, breadcrumbs and chopped tentacles. Cook for 3 minutes, stirring frequently. Take off heat and let mixture cool, then stuff the squid and seal each with a tooth-pick.

In a large, heavy frying pan or casserole, sauté the onions in the remaining olive oil over a low flame until transparent. Pour in wine and water. Simmer slowly for 1 minute and add squid. Cover pan and continue cooking on low heat until squid is done, about 20 minutes. Remove squid and set aside. Turn up heat and reduce liquid to ½ its volume.

Serve squid on rice with sauce poured over it. Try this dish with a dry white wine and an elegant green vegetable, like asparagus.

Estouffade de Calmars aux Poireaux
Squid and Leeks in Red Wine

This is Richard Olney's delicious recipe from his book, Simple French Food.

2 lbs squid, cleaned and cut into rings
The white and pale green parts of 2lbs leeks, cut into 2-inch lengths
¼ cup olive oil
Salt
2 Tbs flour
Pinch cayenne
1 tsp crumbled mixed dry herbs (thyme, oregano. . .)
1 bay leaf
About 8 peeled cloves garlic, sliced paper-thin
About 2 cups red wine
About 1 cup water (2 parts wine to 1 part water in quantity sufficient to cover)
Butter-crisp croutons
Chopped parsley

In a heavy copper *plat á sauter* or a large, low-sided earthenware receptacle large enough to hold the squid and leeks gently packed in a single layer, stew the leeks, salted, in the oil for 10 minutes or so, turning them carefully so as not to damage them, remove them from the pan, and put them aside. Sauté the squid in the same oil, over a higher flame, salted, for several minutes, until the liquid they exude has been almost entirely evaporated, sprinkle over the flour, stir, and cook for another minute or so, add the seasoning, herbs, and garlic, and, stirring all the while, slowly add the red wine, then the water. Bring to a boil, gently slip the leek sections back into the pan, one by one, easing each into place between squid sections. Cook, covered, at a bare simmer, for something over ½ hour—the sauce should be consistent and the squid and leeks of a melting tenderness, but absolutely intact. Scatter the surface with the croutons and chopped parsley at the moment of serving (in the cooking utensil).

Squid Tomato Pasta Sauce

This recipe will sauce at least 4 servings of pasta.

2 lbs squid, cleaned and cut into rings
3 cups canned tomatoes, or 3 lbs raw tomatoes, roughly chopped
1 cup white wine
2-8 cloves garlic, minced
3 Tbs parsley, finely chopped
2 bay leaves
1 tsp sugar
1 can anchovies (optional)
3 Tbs olive oil
Salt and pepper to taste

Sauté garlic in olive oil over low heat in a large casserole or heavy stock pot until lightly browned.

Add canned or raw tomatoes, parsley, bay leaves, sugar, salt and pepper. Over low heat reduce sauce by ⅓. Add white wine and anchovies, if desired. Simmer another 5 minutes. Turn up heat to a moderate boil and add squid. Cook for 3 minutes.

Serve over your favorite pasta accompanied with sour French bread or baguettes and a green salad.

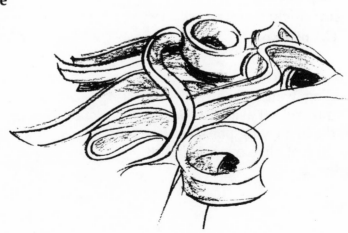

Mary Bruno's Squid Balls

Who could have imagined it, but it's true and they are delicious as an hors d'oeuvre or as an addition to sauces or soup. For a dozen medium-sized squid balls:

2 lbs squid, cleaned and cut into rings
¼ lb cooked shrimp
2 oz each romano and parmesan cheeses, grated
4 cloves garlic, chopped
1 Tb parsley
1 egg yolk
½ cup breadcrumbs
1 cup chicken stock
6 Tbs olive oil

Poach squid rings and tentacles in boiling water for 30 seconds. Drain and set aside to cool. Sauté garlic in a frying pan over low heat in 1 Tb of olive oil until lightly browned.

Combine squid, garlic, the egg yolk and the rest of the dry ingredients in a food processor, using the metal blade attachment. Add 1 or 2 Tbs of olive oil as you go. Stop when the mixture forms a large ball. Remove and form into a dozen or so balls.

Heat 3 Tbs of olive oil in a large, heavy frying pan. When hot, add squid balls and brown on all sides. Turn down heat, add stock, and cover. Simmer for 5 minutes.

Serve hot on toothpicks as is, or accompanied by a dipping sauce such as lemon-garlic butter (see page 40). Mary Bruno uses squid balls as a substitute for meatballs with tomato sauce over pasta.

Squid Cacciuco

This is the Italian variant of the tomato-garlic seafood stew eaten in all of the Mediterranean countries. Many variations are possible. Fish stock can be used in place of red wine. Onion may be included in addition to garlic. Ground fennel seed adds an unexpected twist, and, of course, other seafood may be substituted for part of the squid.

3 lbs squid, cleaned and cut into rings
1 cup red wine
1 cup tomato sauce
1 cup canned tomatoes
2-10 cloves garlic, minced
3 Tbs parsley, chopped
1-4 Tbs olive oil
Salt
Spicy garlic paste (optional)

Sauté garlic in appropriate amount of olive oil in a casserole or heavy stock pot until it is lightly browned. Add the rest of the ingredients except for the squid, and cover.

At this point you have 2 options, depending on your approach to squid. If you like it close to its natural state, that is, firm, you will want to add it to the stew for the last 3 or 4 minutes of cooking, after the liquid has simmered down to a rich, thick stock (about 20 minutes). If you want more tender, but less flavorful squid, add squid 5 minutes after the stew has begun to simmer and cook for 25 minutes or more.

Serve in bowls over toasted sour French bread or baguettes accompanied with spicy garlic paste and a hearty red wine.

SPICY GARLIC PASTE

2-10 cloves garlic, minced
1 boiling potato, cooked
2 large pieces of pimento
Tabasco sauce or cayenne to taste
Olive oil

Combine in a food processor garlic, potato, pimento and tabasco sauce. Add olive oil until it is a thick paste. Serve or store in the refrigerator. It keeps at least 1 week.

Lulas Rechadas
Stuffed Squid

3 lbs squid, cleaned and left whole
¼ lb ham, coarsely chopped
2 hard-boiled eggs, coarsely
 chopped
2 egg yolks
2 cups cooked white rice
2 Tbs parsley, chopped
1 cup canned tomatoes, cut in half
2 onions, finely chopped
4 Tbs olive oil
Salt and pepper to taste

Preheat oven to 350°.

Sauté onions in a frying pan over medium heat until translucent. In a bowl combine ham, hard-boiled eggs, rice, parsley, salt and pepper. Stir in the egg yolks to bind the mixture. Stuff this into the squid with a small spoon. Seal each one with a toothpick. Layer in a baking dish and cover with tomatoes. Bake for 20 minutes.

Serve hot or warm with a green salad and a not too strong red wine.

Calamares en su Tinta
Squid in Its Own Ink

Squid in Its Own Ink is one of the classics of Spanish seafood cooking. Variations are popular in South America and in the Spanish-speaking Caribbean countries.

3 lbs squid, cleaned and cut into rings
14 cloves garlic, finely chopped
¼ cup almonds, ground
2 cups dry white wine
3 Tbs parsley, chopped
1 cup water
Ink from the squid
4 Tbs olive oil
Salt and pepper to taste

Reserve the ink sacs as you clean the squid (see page 18). Put ink sacs into a sieve over a bowl. Break them open with the back of a wooden spoon or spatula. Save the ink which comes through.

In a casserole or heavy stock pot, sauté garlic in olive oil over low heat until lightly browned. Add almond paste and continue cooking slowly for 2 minutes. Moisten with a little of the water if necessary to prevent sticking. Now add white wine, ink, parsley, salt and pepper. Slowly simmer covered for 25 minutes.

Uncover, turn up heat to a moderate boil, and add squid. Simmer for 3 minutes. (You may, of course, cook the squid for 25 minutes, as in the other stew recipes.)

Serve immediately over rice accompanied by a dry white wine and a green salad.

Calamares Rellenos con Jamón
Squid Stuffed with Smoked Ham

This is a favorite of British seafood scholar Alan Davidson. It appears in his book Mediterranean Seafood. *The English have only taken to eating squid fairly recently, so the definitive English approach to squid has yet to appear. Who knows? Squid and chips just might become a staple.*

2 lbs squid, cleaned and left whole

4 oz smoked ham

2 or 3 ripe tomatoes, peeled

Parsley, chopped

1 large onion, chopped

2 cloves garlic, whole

Salt and pepper to taste

4 Tbs oil

Chop the tentacles very finely together with the ham and 2 tomatoes. Add salt and pepper and a little chopped parsley. The mixture should be quite thick. Stuff the squid with it, but not quite full and fasten each with a toothpick.

Cook the chopped onion gently in oil with 2 cloves of garlic, whole. Add another tomato if you wish. When the ingredients have blended well together put the squid in and cook for 20 minutes over low heat. Add a little water (or wine) if the sauce is drying up towards the end of the cooking.

ASIAN RECIPES

CHINA

*Stir-Fried Squid with Peanuts
  and Chiles*
Yao Bao Saung Yao
Black Bean Sauce Squid
Stir-Fried Squid with Curry
Chinese Squid Salad
Chinese Squid Balls

JAPAN

Squid Teryaki
Squid Misoyaki
Squid Ball Soup

THAILAND

Thai Spicy Squid Salad
Squid Sate
Squid with Oyster Sauce and Basil

INDONESIA

Squid Curried in Coconut Milk
Squid Sambal

PHILIPPINES

Adobong Pusit

POLYNESIA

Stuffed Squid Soup

INTRODUCTION TO ASIAN RECIPES

China

Chinese gastronomy is an integral part of Chinese social life. The habits and customs of the Chinese are inscribed into their cooking, often in the names of the dishes.

The name for stir-fried squid has a particularly amusing origin. In old China when an employee was hired, he went to live with his employer. Naturally he brought his bedroll. When he was fired, he rolled up his bedding and left. This action reminded the Chinese of the squid as it rolled up in the wok. And so the written symbol which signifies being fired also has come to mean stir-fried squid.

The Chinese cook with dry rice wine. Dry sherry is an acceptable substitute. Mirin, Japanese sweet rice wine, may also be used. Just add less sugar.

In order to seal in the flavor of fresh ingredients Chinese cooks blanch vegetables and some shellfish in boiling water for a few seconds just before they stir-fry them. Blanching gives squid an extra firmness. Try it for all the Asian sautés and you may end up blanching all the squid you fry.

Japan

The Japanese catch and eat more squid than any other people in the world. They have a multitude of ways to prepare squid, some of them by now familiar to Westerners, others still quite exotic.

The waters around Japan yield at least half a dozen varieties of squid. One of the larger species is available, cleaned and frozen, in some cities. It is excellent for barbecuing and, because it is so large, for stuffing.

Thailand

Thai cooking is a marvelous blend of Chinese and Indian influences. Some of the dishes are curried, others stir-fried using Chinese sauces, and many are mysterious blends using local ingredients.

Stir-Fried Squid with Peanuts and Chiles

In traditional Chinese cooking, dishes which are part of a banquet-style meal usually contain about 1 pound of food. This dish will serve 4 if there are 3 other dishes besides soup; 6 if there are 6 other dishes, etc.

1 lb squid, cleaned Chinese-style (see page 22)

¼ cup raw peanuts, roughly chopped

4 cloves garlic, minced

1 or more fresh chile peppers, chopped

1 tsp cilantro, chopped (optional)

2 tsps soy sauce

¼ cup chicken stock

1 tsp cornstarch dissolved in 1 Tb stock or water

3-4 Tbs vegetable oil

Sauté garlic and chile peppers in half the oil over low heat in a wok or heavy frying pan until garlic is lightly browned. Add peanuts for the last 30 seconds. Stir continuously.

Remove ingredients from the pan, add more oil, if necessary, and the squid. Cook for 30 seconds. Return peanuts, garlic and chiles to pan. Immediately add all but 1 Tb of the stock, soy sauce and cilantro. Continue stir-frying for another minute. Add cornstarch mixture. When sauce thickens, remove from heat and serve.

Yao Bao Saung Yao
Oil Exploded
Double Squid

This unusually-titled dish features dried and fresh squid. Dried squid is a very common food in China and in Hong Kong where it is eaten as a snack, the way Westerners eat beef jerky. It is also used as a flavoring and as a food in cooked dishes. Dried squid takes a little getting used to, but does not taste as strange as it looks. It is available in Asian grocery stores and Chinatowns.

1 lb squid, cleaned Chinese-style
4 oz dried squid
½ inch ginger, thinly sliced
2-6 cloves garlic, minced
Vegetable oil for stir-frying
2 tsps sesame oil
Salt to taste
1 tsp baking soda
1 tsp sugar

Soak dried squid in water with the baking soda for 30 minutes.

Blanch the fresh and the dried squid in boiling water for just a few seconds. Do not cook completely. Drain and pat dry. Heat the vegetable oil in a wok or large frying pan. When it is very hot, add all the squid. Remove after 30 seconds. Add more oil to the wok if necessary, and heat. Cook the squid and all the remaining ingredients over high heat for about a minute. Remove from the wok, drizzle with sesame oil, and serve with rice.

As a main dish this recipe serves 2. As a side dish, 4 or more.

Black Bean Sauce Squid

Many people shy away from dishes with names like Black Bean Sauce Squid because they think it involves the preparation of a complicated sauce. In fact it is quite easy. The black beans themselves, fermented and salted when you buy them, are the sauce. All you do is add a little rice wine to make a paste. Then it's just like any other stir-fry—a couple of minutes of high-heat cooking, continuous stirring, and the dish is done.

1 lb squid, cleaned Chinese-style (see page 22)
2 Tbs fermented, salted black beans (available at Asian groceries)
2 cloves garlic, minced
2 Tbs rice wine, or 2 Tbs mirin or sherry
1 tsp ginger, grated
2 scallions, chopped into ½-inch pieces
1 Tb regular soy sauce
1 tsp sugar
1 tsp cornstarch dissolved in 1 Tb water
2 Tbs vegetable oil

Prepare black bean sauce mixture by adding to the beans: rice wine, soy sauce and sugar. Let sit for 15 minutes.

Sauté garlic and ginger in the oil over medium heat in a heavy frying pan or wok until garlic is slightly browned. Turn up heat. Add squid and scallions. Stir-fry for 30 seconds. Pour in black bean sauce mixture, and cook for 2 minutes. Add cornstarch and, when sauce thickens, remove from heat and serve.

Stir-Fried Squid with Curry

2 lbs squid, cleaned and cut into pieces Chinese-style (page 22)
2 green bell peppers, sliced
1 onion, chopped
2 tsps curry powder
2 tsps vinegar
½ cup chicken stock or water
2 tsps cornstarch dissolved in 2 Tbs water
4 Tbs vegetable oil
Salt to taste

In a large, heavy frying pan or a wok, sauté the onions and peppers over low heat until the onions are translucent. Add the curry powder, stir and heat another minute. Pour in the stock or water, vinegar, salt and the squid. Turn up the heat and cook everything for 3 minutes. Add cornstarch mixture. When the sauce thickens, remove from heat and serve.

As a side dish this recipe serves 6-8; as a main course, 3.

Chinese Squid Salad

2 lbs squid, cleaned Chinese-style (see page 22)
2 green bell peppers, chopped
4 Tbs regular soy sauce
1 Tb white vinegar
1 Tb rice wine, or 1 Tb sherry
2 Tbs vegetable oil
1 Tb sesame oil (there is no substitute for sesame oil)
1 tsp sugar

Blanch squid 30 seconds in boiling water. Drain and set aside to cool. Sauté bell peppers in oil in a frying pan over low heat until soft. Combine squid and peppers in a bowl. Mix together soy sauce, wine, vinegar and sesame oil. Pour this over squid and peppers. Refrigerate.

Serve cold or at room temperature as the first course of a Chinese meal.

Chinese Squid Balls

2 lbs squid, cleaned and cut into rings
½ lb cooked shrimp
4 cloves garlic, chopped
1 Tb cilantro, chopped
1 egg yolk
½ cup water chestnuts, chopped
1 cup chicken stock
1 Tb ginger, grated
6 Tbs peanut oil

Poach squid rings and tentacles in boiling water for 30 seconds. Drain and set aside to cool.

Sauté garlic in a frying pan over low heat in 1 Tb of oil until lightly browned.

Combine squid, garlic, the egg yolk and the rest of the dry ingredients in a food processor. Add 1 or 2 Tbs of oil as you go. Stop when the mixture forms a large ball. Remove and form into a dozen or so balls. Heat 3 Tbs of oil in a large, heavy frying pan. When hot, add squid balls and brown lightly on all sides. Turn down heat, add stock, and cover. Simmer for five minutes.

Serve on toothpicks with soy sauce, or use as fish balls in soup, or as an addition to Stuffed Squid Soup (page 71).

Squid Teryaki

**3 lbs squid, cleaned and cut into
  rings**
½ cup soy sauce
½ cup mirin, or ½ cup sherry
½ cup water
2 Tbs sugar
1 tsp cornstarch
Juice of 2 lemons

To make the teryaki sauce, combine all the ingredients except the cornstarch. Reserve half of the sauce, marinate the squid in the other half for 1 hour.

Prepare the fire (see page 44).

Skewer squid pieces and tentacles.

Heat the reserved teryaki sauce in a saucepan. When it begins to boil, add the cornstarch dissolved in a little water. As soon as the sauce thickens, remove from heat. As it cooks you will baste the squid with this teryaki sauce.

Grill the squid until it turns dark brown, 2-3 minutes per side, depending on the heat, and then turn it over. Baste one last time and then remove skewers from the fire. Serve over rice accompanied with any remaining sauce.

Squid Misoyaki

Miso is fermented soybean paste, a staple in Japanese and Chinese cooking. It comes in a variety of tastes and colors. Brown miso is fine for squid, but the other varieties will do just about as well.

3 lbs squid, cleaned and cut into rings
½ cup miso
3 Tbs mirin, or 3 Tbs sherry and ½ tsp sugar
2 Tbs sugar or more to taste
4 Tbs sesame seeds or, if that is unavailable, wheat germ

Prepare the fire (see page 44) and skewer the squid.

Combine mirin, sugar and miso paste. Cover the squid with miso mixture and the sesame seeds.

Grill 2-3 minutes on each side, depending on the temperature of the fire. When the squid browns, turn it over. Add more paste and grill again until brown. Remove and serve.

Squid Ball Soup

The Japanese usually like their soups to be delicate. This is a hearty soup which, with a few additions, could become a meal. This recipe makes a dozen small balls and serves 6.

1½ lbs squid, cleaned and cut into rings
1 tsp ginger, grated
6 cups Dashi No Moto (fish stock base available dried or in bags which is combined with water), or other clear stock
1 Tbs cornstarch
Water
Salt to taste
2 carrots, thinly sliced
2 scallions, chopped

Blanch squid pieces for 30 seconds in boiling water. Combine with cornstarch and ginger in a food processor. Slowly add water until the mixture forms a very thick paste, as coarse as ground hamburger. Form into balls. Steam for 5 minutes over boiling water.

Bring the Dashi No Moto or stock to a boil. Add squid balls. Simmer for 5 minutes. Add carrots and scallions. Cook 2 minutes longer. Serve accompanied with soy sauce.

To make this soup more substantial, include 1 or 2 large pieces of tofu cut into small squares to be added along with the squid and a large bunch of spinach, chopped into small pieces. This is cooked along with the other vegetables.

Thai Spicy Squid Salad

This recipe and the other Thai recipes which follow are the work of Somchai Aksombon, co-owner and head chef at Siam Cuisine in Berkeley, California. Somchai, or Chai as he is known, is a squid lover: his regular menu features no less than 6 different squid dishes and squid specials are frequent. This recipe serves 6 as an appetizer.

2 lbs squid, cleaned and cut into rings
3 Tbs fish sauce (available at Asian groceries)
2 tsps fresh ginger, finely minced
Juice of 2 limes
3 or 4 stalks of cilantro (Chinese parsley) or 2 Tbs fresh mint, chopped
2 Tbs fresh Thai or Italian basil, chopped (see page 67)
½ purple onion, thinly sliced
Lettuce
Cayenne to taste

Immerse squid in boiling water for 30 seconds. Remove and drain. Set aside to cool.

Combine fish sauce, lime juice, ginger and cayenne. Layer a plate with large lettuce leaves. Add squid, cilantro, basil and purple onion. Pour sauce over salad and serve immediately.

You will want to drink beer with this dish, especially if you have been generous with the cayenne.

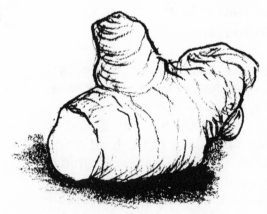

Squid Sate
Barbecued Squid with Hot Dipping Sauce

This dish serves 4-6 as part of a larger meal.

2 lbs squid, cleaned and cut into rings
1 cup coconut milk
2 cloves garlic, chopped
6 Tbs fish sauce (available at Asian groceries)
3 Tbs peanuts, finely chopped
Juice of 1 lime
Cayenne to taste
1 tsp sugar

Coconut milk is easily made if you have a blender or food processor. Boil 1½ cups water. Pour it over 1½ cups of fresh or dry grated coconut. Beat it in the food processor or blender for at least 1 minute. Strain it through a sieve or through cheesecloth. Marinate the squid for 1 hour in coconut milk to which you have added the garlic.

Prepare the coals (see page 44) and skewer the squid.

To make the dipping sauce which makes this dish so distinctive, combine the fish sauce, peanuts, sugar, lime juice and the cayenne.

Grill the squid about 3 minutes on each side. When brown, turn over and barbecue 3 minutes more.

Serve accompanied by the dipping sauce.

This recipe will produce tasty grilled fish if you use firm varieties such as swordfish, sea bass or halibut, cutting the steaks or fillets into large squares.

Squid with Oyster Sauce and Basil

This dish is probably Chinese in origin. Its distinctive flavor comes from a variety of basil grown in Thailand which is not generally available in this country. In order to ensure himself a supply, Chai of Siam Cuisine grows it in a little plot behind his restaurant. If you don't have a source for this wonderful herb, use Italian basil. The taste is quite different but it is still very good. This dish serves 4-6 as a side dish.

2 lbs squid, cleaned and cut into rings
2 or more cloves garlic, minced
2 Tbs oyster sauce (available at many supermarkets and at Asian groceries)
1 Tbs basil, fresh only
1 Tbs fish sauce
Water
Vegetable oil
1 or more finely chopped fresh hot chiles (Thai dishes are hot!)

Sauté chile peppers and garlic in oil in a large, heavy frying pan over low heat until garlic is lightly browned.

Add the oyster and fish sauces and a little water. Bring to a boil and add squid. Turn up heat and cook for a minute. Include basil, cook 2 minutes longer. If the sauce is too thick, add a little water.

Serve immediately with rice.

Squid Curried in Coconut Milk

In the East, curries are not made with curry powder but with a combination of spices suited to the food being cooked. Turmeric is the main curry spice in this dish, along with ample amounts of ginger, garlic and onions. Of course, you may experiment, adding other spices if you like. Ground coriander seeds add a nice touch. And in the same vein, a few ground fennel seeds would also be appropriate. This recipe makes a side dish for 4-6.

2 lbs squid, cleaned, cut into rings
2 cups coconut milk (see page 66)
3-8 cloves garlic, minced
1 tsp ginger, grated
1 onion, finely chopped
4 Tbs tamarind juice made from
  1 tsp of tamarind extract (see
  page 40), or 2 Tbs lemon juice
4 Tbs peanuts, chopped
1 or more fresh chile peppers,
  chopped
1 tsp turmeric
Vegetable oil

In a food processor or blender combine the turmeric, ginger, peanuts and garlic. When it forms a stiff paste, set it aside.

In a large, heavy frying pan sauté the onions and chile peppers over low heat until the onions are translucent. Add the spice paste, tamarind juice, and immediately thereafter, the coconut milk. Simmer the sauce, uncovered, until it becomes thick. Add the squid, turn up the heat to a moderate boil, and cook for 3 minutes.

Serve over rice accompanied by condiments such as roasted peanuts, toasted coconut and hot sauce.

Squid Sambal

This dish has several unusual ingredients for which there are adequate substitutes available. In any case, all the exotic ingredients are available at a Chinese grocery.

2 lbs squid, cleaned and cut into
   rings
1 onion, chopped
¼ cup almonds
2 fresh chiles, finely chopped, or
   1 tsp cayenne
1 tsp grated lemon peel
1 tsp tamarind concentrate,
   dissolved in 2 Tbs water,
   or 2 Tbs lemon juice
1 tsp lemon grass (dry), or 1 stalk
   fresh lemon grass, chopped
1 Tbs brown sugar
¼ tsp shrimp paste (known as
   shrimp sauce in China), or 1 tsp
   dried, salted shrimp
2 Tbs vegetable oil

In a food processor, purée the onion, almonds, chiles and shrimp paste.

In a large, heavy frying pan or a wok, sauté the spice paste in oil over low heat. When it turns dark brown, add tamarind water, the lemon, lemon grass and sugar. Sauté a minute more, then add the squid. Turn up the heat and cook for 3 minutes, adding water if necessary to keep the sauce from sticking. Remove from heat and serve over rice.

As a main course this dish serves 3; as a side dish, 6 or more.

Adobong Pusit
Squid Adobo

3 lbs squid, cleaned and cut into
   rings
10 or more cloves garlic, minced
¾ cups vinegar
2 cups water
2 tomatoes, thinly sliced
2 onions, thinly sliced
Soy sauce to taste
3 Tbs vegetable oil

Sauté garlic in oil over low heat in a large frying pan or wok until lightly browned.

Add soy sauce, vinegar and water. Turn up to high heat and boil down for a minute. Now add squid, tomatoes, and onions. Cook for 2 to 3 minutes, then remove squid, tomatoes, and onions from the pan. Keep warm. Turn heat all the way up and boil down the sauce until it thickens. Pour over squid and vegetables.

Serve with rice.

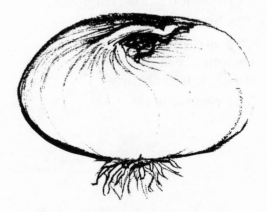

Stuffed Squid Soup

The squid is a favorite food in Asia, in part because it can be substituted for nonseafood ingredients, such as wontons, creating a pleasant variation on a classic theme. This recipe serves 6 as a first course.

1½ lbs squid, cleaned and left
   whole
½ lb pork, ground
1 tsp ginger, grated
1-2 tsps soy sauce, according to
   taste
1 tsp cilantro, chopped
1 quart chicken stock

Combine pork, ginger, cilantro and soy sauce. Stuff squid with this mixture using a pastry bag (see page 23). Seal each with a toothpick.

Bring chicken stock to a slow boil in a stock pot. Add the squid and cook for 7 or 8 minutes.

Serve hot with soy sauce on the side.

Variation:

To make a more substantial soup, include squid balls (page 61), mushrooms and, if you like, spinach.

Squid Fishing in Monterey

N et fishing was imported to the Monterey Bay by Sicilian immigrants in the 1870s. They gravitated to the temperate waters of the Bay located just south of San Francisco, because it reminded them of their native country: protected and generally calm except during the winter storms. So many Sicilians moved to Monterey that by 1900 the city was inhabited almost entirely by Mexicans and Italians.

They brought with them their traditional style of fishing—lampara. Lampara fishing was done at night using a bright light to attract the catch into the net. The net was pulled in by hand; often twelve men crowded onto a thirty-foot sailboat to hoist the cotton net which became incredibly heavy with the weight of water and fish. The diesel engine replaced the sail around the turn of the century, but it wasn't until 1946 that the mechanical gurdy was introduced. Vince Bruno, a young Monterey fisherman who got tired of breaking his back night after night, hooked up half of the rear end of an automobile to the boat's main drive shaft. He covered the steel disc with rubber so that it would not shred the net as it rotated. The labor of twelve men was now done by a crew of four or five, using two gurdies. Nylon nets were introduced in the late forties. They tear less easily and save the fishermen the work of drying the nets, necessary to prevent the cotton rotting from the bacteria which live in the kelp, bits of fish, and debris which sticks to the mesh.

Until sardine fishing stopped after World War II, squid were caught on a limited basis, and then only for export. During the twenties, squid were taken directly from the boats in trucks to a field near the Monterey airport—Fisherman Flats—where several tons were spread out to dry over twenty-four acres of bare ground. At the end of a week, the squid were raked up, dirt, bugs and all, and shipped to China where they were further preserved and sold as a delicacy.

When the sardines disappeared from the Bay* most of the Monterey fleet of seventy seiners switched over to squid. Of sixteen Monterey canneries and ten at Moss Landing, fifteen converted to squid; the rest closed down. The industry staggered back onto its feet.

Today there are two seiners and a dozen smaller boats fishing for squid. One cannery operates at Moss Landing.

The actual fishing process has changed little since it was brought from Italy except for the introduction of more modern equipment. The boats leave the harbor and head towards the squid's breeding grounds a couple of hundred yards off the beach at Pacific Grove or near Cannery Row. They cruise around slowly with the crew standing at the bow peering intently into the dark water. The schools are spotted by the phosphorescent trails they stir up as they swim through the sea. (Each species of fish leaves a distinct pattern of light, varying according to its size, its speed and the manner in which it swims.) On the bridge, the captain checks his sonar meter which registers the depth of the school. He makes an intuitive judgment as to the school's size. If he decides to set, he maneuvers his boat into position so that he can encircle the maximum number of fish. This is a complicated and tricky process, because the tide, depth of the ocean, and the wind all influence the movement of the school as well as the shape of the net after it enters

*The two theories on this infamous natural disaster are, of course, conflicting. The fishermen point to the introduction of pesticides in the Salinas Valley whose rivers empty into the Bay. Whereas others, including farmers, blame the rapid decline of the sardine population on over-fishing.

the water. At just the right moment the skipper yells down to his crew members to release the net. First, a wooden pole fitted with a red light is fastened to the end of the wing. This light allows the captain atop the flying bridge to see where to place the net, and it also warns the other boats so that they will not set in the same place or run over the net. Coiled in three piles at the back of the boat, the net is let out by two men, one who regulates the speed of its release, allowing for the movement of the sea, and a second who separates the lead line from the corks. The two men who let out the net wear rubber arm guards made from wet suits to protect their arms from the cutting mesh as it rapidly slides over their equally rapidly moving limbs. It is difficult to wear gloves as one loses a feel for the mesh which is essential to stacking and pulling the net. For many fishermen the net is an almost spiritual object, to be treated with all the reverence due to such a powerful and helpful force. Aside from the fact that the nets are very expensive and tear easily, they are the fisherman's contact with the sea—a little bit of man and a little bit of nature—and thus thought of more as an extension of his arm than as a piece of equipment. The net is referred to in conversation almost like another crew member, and in fact usually gets one share of the catch for its efforts.

When fully extended, each 100-yard long wing reaches down about ten fathoms—sixty feet. After the first wing is let out, the sack, a U-shaped bag of fine mesh forty yards in length, is pushed over. As soon as the other wing is released the fish are encircled except for a narrow opening underneath the boat.

Two men fit the net onto the winches. They pull and stack it at their feet in one continuous motion, often punctuated by the shouts of other fishermen who are checking the net as it comes out of the water for sharks, jelly fish, star fish or seaweed which might tangle up the winches. The net must be taken off both gurdies each time such an obstacle is removed, so that the mesh may be carefully untangled.

As the circle of the net tightens, the squid sense it. They bunch together and swim around confusedly. When it nears the surface, trying to escape, the school stirs up the phosphorus, illuminating the sea and even casting a glow onto the area around the boat. The men stamp on the deck as the squid in their panic near the opening underneath the boat. The air is filled with the sweet smell of the fish, a pungent aroma similar to that of wet grass.

The sack, which by now holds all the fish, is pulled in by hand. The men strain to get the lead line in the center of the sack; when it is on board the catch is encircled. Often the squid, sensing danger, dive to the bottom, necessitating the use of a block and tackle (which is rigged to the boom) to hoist up the tons of sinking weight. When the sack is drawn up so that little water remains, the fish are brailed (scooped) into the hold or into an empty skiff which is pulled behind during fishing.

After the net is emptied, it is restacked and the process is repeated until the litter (or hold, if it is a bigger boat) is full, or until dawn's light ends the effectiveness of the lampara technique. Seven or eight sets may be necessary to load up, though occasionally, with a little luck, one set will yield twenty tons.

Squid live all along the West coast, though they exist in concentration sufficient for fishing only in the Monterey Bay and around the Channel Islands off Southern California. In the south they are caught by more modern methods. A bright light attracts the squid which are brought onto the boat by a telescoping suction pipe whose depth is regulated by the sonar fathometer. This style of fishing has been outlawed in the Monterey Bay through the lobbying efforts of the local

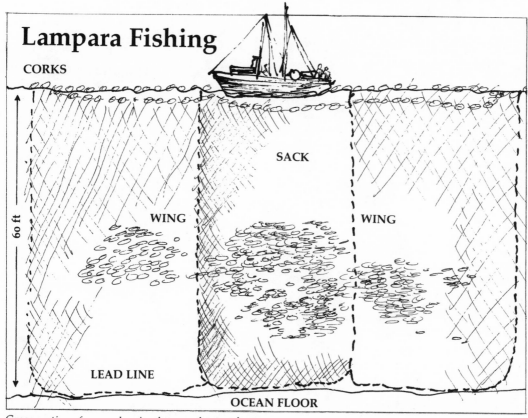

Cross section of ocean showing lampara boat and net.

Fisherman's Union. In the north, the season usually lasts from March or April to November, both because that is when the squid are most frequently in the Bay, and because lampara fishing requires relatively calm seas.

In the Bay there is not usually a restriction placed on squid fishing, although the eggs and the size of the squid caught are monitored by the Fish and Game Department to ensure a sufficient number to maintain the area's population.

The Giant Squid — Fact

Yes, giant squids exist and not only in literature and mythology. The giant squid, or kraken as it is most commonly called, is the world's largest invertebrate, reaching a size of at least 60 feet, including the tentacles. It inhabits many, if not all, of the world's oceans and generally lives a peaceful life, though it will attack if it is challenged. For some unexplained reason a rash of kraken were encountered off the coast of Newfoundland during

the 1870s. A photograph of a kraken lying draped over the bathtub of a local minister provides undeniable evidence of the existence of the species. The same locale also produced at least one documented giant squid attack. Two men and a boy were out fishing for herring in a small rowboat when they caught sight of what looked like the wreckage of a ship floating on the surface of the water. When they poked it with their boat hook, the kraken attacked. The men froze with fear, but the young boy, keeping his cool, cut the tentacles which grasped the boat and the kraken retreated. The boy became a local hero and sold the severed tentacle—19 feet long—to a local naturalist for a handsome price.

Though kraken encounters with men are extremely rare, its meetings with the sperm whale are not so infrequent, an unfortunate fact for the giant squid which inevitably loses these battles. In his book, *Voyage of the Cachalot*, Frank Bullen, a British sailor and writer, describes the titanic struggle between whale and squid. The year is 1875, the place is the Indian Ocean.

Bullen was on watch one night; and he tells us that he "was so tired and sleepy that I knew not how to keep awake. I did not imagine that anything would happen to make me prize that night's experience for the rest of my life, or I should have taken matters with a far better grace.

"At about 11 PM, I was leaning over the lee rail, gazing steadily at the bright surface of the sea, where the intense radiance of the tropical moon made a broad path like a pavement of burnished silver. Eyes that saw not, mind only confusedly conscious of my surrounds, were mine; but suddenly I started to my feet with an exclamation, and stared with all my might at the strangest sight I ever saw. There was a violent commotion in the sea right where the moon's rays were concentrated, so great that, remembering our position, I was at first inclined to alarm all hands; for I had often heard of volcanic islands suddenly lifting their heads from the depths below, or disappearing in a moment, and, with Sumatra's chain of active volcanoes so near, I felt doubtful indeed of what was now happening.

"Getting the night-glasses out of the cabin scuttle, where they were always hung in readiness, I focused them on the troubled spot, perfectly satisfied by a short examination that neither volcano nor earthquake had anything to do with what was going on; yet so vast were the forces engaged that I might well have been excused for my first supposition. A very large sperm whale was locked in deadly conflict with a cuttlefish, or squid, almost as large as himself, whose interminable tentacles seemed to enlace the whole of his great body. The head of the whale especially seemed a perfect net-work of writhing arms—naturally, I suppose, for it appeared as if the whale had the tail part of the mollusc in his jaws, and, in a business-like, methodical way, was sawing through it.

"By the side of the black columnar head of the whale appeared the head of a great squid, as awful an object as one could well imagine even in a fevered dream. Judging as carefully as possible, I estimated it to be at least as large as one of our pipes, which contained three hundred and fifty gallons; but it may have been, and probably was, a good deal larger. The eyes were very remarkable from the size and blackness, which, contrasted with the vivid whiteness of the head, made their appearance all the more striking. They were, at least, a foot in diameter, and, seen under such conditions, looked decidedly eery and hobgoblin-like.

"All around the combatants were numerous sharks, like jackals round a lion, ready to share the feast, and apparently assisting in the destruction of the huge cephalopod. So the titanic struggle went on, in perfect silence as far as we were concerned, because, even had there been any noise, our distance from the scene of conflict would not have permitted us to hear it.

"Thinking that such a sight ought not to be missed by the captain, I overcame my dread of him sufficiently to call him, and tell him of what was taking place. He met my remarks with such a furious burst of anger at my daring to disturb him for such a cause that I fled precipitately on deck again, having the remainder of the vision to myself. . . The conflict ceased, the sea resumed its placid calm, and nothing remained to tell of the fight but a strong odor of fish, as of a bank of seaweed left by the tide in the blazing sun."

Today, Fred Aldrich, a marine biologist living in Newfoundland, thinks the giant squid are still more likely to be found in his part of the ocean. Other scientists disagree. They think the kraken are everywhere and nowhere in particular. One thing is certain, in our era where many unusual species have become instant celebrities, the next time a kraken sighting is substantiated, we will all hear about it.

The Squid Theory of History

*any of the world's greatest works of litera-
ture remain hidden from public view,
rejected by their authors, or more commonly by publishers, who often lack the
courage to print what is new and con-
troversial. Such a book is* The Squid
Theory of History *written by Loligo
Pealeii in 1514. The Milanese Pealeii had,
it appears from his book, a most original
and peculiar viewpoint on world events.
He held that all of the important events
in mankind's history were influenced by
none other than the squid. While Pealeii
granted that man makes his own destiny,
the course of events, he affirmed, is none
the less altered by the presence of the squid.
After an exhaustive study, Pealeii, like the early Polynesians, concluded that the
squid and octopus were the primordial creatures which had crawled out of the
sea to bring life to earth. Thus all terrestrial life was indebted to the squid for its
existence. Beyond this, Pealeii saw the squid's presence as being essential to the
dawn of civilization. The Greeks gave their infants the squid as a gift on the fifth
day after birth. The cephalopod, with its strong grasping power, insured that
the baby would quickly acquire the power to grab and to walk. Pealeii logically
reasoned that the inquisitiveness and perspicacity of the Greeks was due to their
early introduction to the squid. He even traced the origin of tidal waves, which
occasionally ravaged the sea coast cities of the Mediterranean, to the squid. From
observations of the Phoenicians, he learned that tidal waves were often preceded
by the sighting of a colossal struggle between a sperm whale and a giant squid.*

Didn't it follow then that the violent surge of water must be the result of its displacement by the battling titans? One could continue at great length to cite the evidence Pealeii drew on. Here, however, it may be more appropriate to cite a section of the work which most amused me, a marvelous story.

Pealeii's story begins in Northern Italy in the year 1514. Duke Ludovico Allessandro was at war with his rival Count Ramiro Lorenzo. They had waged a bitter but inconclusive struggle for fifteen years. By now each side had erected elaborate defenses suited to prolonged warfare. the parapets, trenches and towers of the two rival kingdoms stood a few hundred yards apart with a scarred no man's land between them. Finally, out of desperation, Allessandro decided to ask his neighbor to the North, Count Giuseppe Ammanato, for assistance. They met in a cafe frequented by seamen on the waterfront of Genoa. Their conversation was interrupted by a wild-eyed youth who noisily boasted he had seen a giant squid twenty miles southwest of Genoa. The two men laughed at the exaggerated gestures of the young sailor and returned to their discourse. The Duke gradually brought the conversation around to the war he was waging and to his need for additional troops. Count Ammanato politely declined to lend his support, citing his lack of confidence in the Duke as an organizer. And there the matter stands when we take up Pealeii's narrative. The account, which is here excerpted and condensed for obvious reasons, is indeed a remarkable history. I leave it to the reader to judge its authenticity.

he Duke's fleet regularly fished the waters of the Mediterranean, providing his subjects with an abundant variety of seafood—shrimp, lobster, cod, perch, mullett, octopus and bass found their way to his affluent table. A week after the Anchor Inn meeting of Ammanato and Allessandro, the waterfront was still alive with discussion of the giant squid. So when Ammanato's fishermen found their net to be a little more difficult to pull in than usual, they jokingly suggested it had become their fate to land the giant creature. Imagine the amazement of the skeptics on board when they saw a column of black liquid shoot one hundred feet into the air. For ten minutes no other sign of life surfaced; the fishermen's terror gradually gave way to their curiosity. The men, struggling now against an immense weight, slowly pulled up the net to reveal a squid some ninety feet long lying inert and easily visible in the clear water. Its ten arms, or rather feet, fixed to its head were twice as long as its body and were twisted like a bramble bush. One could see the two hundred and fifty airholes on the inner side of the tentacles. The monster's mouth, a horned beak like a parrot's, opened and shut vertically. Its tongue, a rough texture, furnished with several rows of pointed teeth, came out quivering from this veritable pair of shears. Its spindle-like body formed a fleshy mass that must have weighed 4,000 to 5,000 pounds. The varying color changed with great rapidity; according to the irritation of the animal, it passed successively from livid gray to reddish brown. The eyes of the squid were still alert and showed an intelligence that seemed almost human.

All thirty crew members were needed to pull the shiny hulk over the rail and onto the deck. When one curious fisherman pulled the tentacles apart to have a better look at the horned beak he was toppled by a powerful spray of black ink from the near dead beast.

A messenger was immediately dispatched to bring the bizarre news to the castle five miles inland. When Allessandro heard of the extraordinary incident, he rubbed his hands together with great satisfaction; the wild-

eyed youth had been right. Chance had granted him an opportunity to win over Ammanato.

Duke Allessandro assembled his servants and proudly announced to them that they would be preparing the first giant squid feast in the history of Italy (and probably in the history of the world)—a feat of no little difficulty.

First the Duke ordered his masons to construct a giant brick oven (all of these preparations had to be made with the greatest haste to assure completion before the squid became inedible). They had developed their art building fortifications for Allessandro's army. The stones and mortar stockpiled for emergencies were well suited to the massive construction required. Used to working without plans or precise measurement, the masons improvised on the spot. Clambering over their bamboo scaffolding like monkeys, with loads of stone and mortar in sacks strapped to their backs, the masons chipped and cut, trowled and tamped until they had erected the perfect receptacle for the giant cephalopod. The completed oven was arch-shaped and gracefully proportioned. It stood twenty feet high and measured forty feet in length. A huge shelf, under which the fire would burn, ran the length of the chamber. The blaze would be fed from the outside by means of a tunnel which ran from the shelf to the exterior wall. A supply of hardwood, several trees worth, was stacked beside the oven as soon as it was finished.

In the meantime, the carpenters had fashioned the platform on which the cooking squid would rest. While its total length exceeded that of the animal by several feet, it was segmented in order to permit sectioning the squid after cooking but before it was transported to the Prince's table. The wood had been thoroughly soaked so that it would not burn during the lengthy cooking process.

By the time the squid arrived, transported on three carts with long planks stretching between them, the wooden platform was near completion. Thirty strong men, equipped with many belts, pulleys and levers, slid the squid onto the platform. The tentacles, which had become stiff, were severed with many blows of a huge axe. This exhausted half a dozen stout lads as the foot-thick appendages were of an unusual resiliency. The cooks then inserted duelling pikes into the squid's head. Ropes were strung from the pikes to a team of four powerful horses, who sweated and strained until they had pulled out the head and the guts attached to it. The clear plastic pen (or backbone) was carefully removed and saved for later use. Washing out the body cavity completed the preliminary preparations.

In order to keep the hollow body of the squid from collapsing, the carpenters next inserted vertical wood beams. These were taken out as the stuffing progressed. Ladders were set on either side of the squid. Two cooks sewed shut the internal cavity using a two-foot piece of sharpened ivory through which a hole had been pierced and a long length of rope attached. Passing the ivory needle back and forth, they worked their way quickly up the ladders. When the sealing process was finished, the squid, on its cooking rack, was slid into the oven.

The preparations for the feast were nearly as elaborate as those of the oven construction. Allessandro invited one hundred of the local gentry to the dinner, including amongst the guests those of his subjects most skilled in the arts of lively humor and conversation. Several chamber groups were hired, as well as strolling lutists who would be serenading the guests with songs at their request. An enormous store of mead, ale and wine had been laid aside, filling the Prince's storehouse to over-flowing.

The Count arrived at dusk on horseback, accompanied by two of his lieutenants. He greeted Allessandro with a certain reserve, unsure of the latter's intentions. The Duke mentioned nothing of his previous request and quickly put Ammanato at ease with some witty remarks about the local bishop, whom both men found to be a buffoon of the highest order. The nobles and their friends were soon engaged in a merry round of joking and drinking.

The opening air of a familiar dance turned everyone's attention to the center of the hall. A gay troupe of dancers, drunk with the wine given them by the kitchen help, circled madly as the musicians, catching their spirit, increased the tempo. Running to keep up with the music, they collided and collapsed into a laughing heap.

The servants had been ordered to bring in the first course as soon as the music ended. They gingerly threaded their way through the sprawling bodies, balancing trays piled high with marzipan, prosciutto cooked in wine, salted pork tongues and sliced spit-roasted songbirds covered in aspic and artfully arranged to form a giant hawk.

When the plates had been cleared away, Allessandro turned to the Count and spoke: "You will agree with me, I think that tonight's dinner proved somewhat unusual. In fact, I venture to say it is probably the first time any man has been served such a meal." Ammanato, earlier distracted, was now looking directly at the Count.

A fanfare of trumpets and a roll of the drums announced the arrival of the giant squid, still whole, into the Duke's dining room. The cooking platform had been reassembled and placed on carts now drawn by the kitchen helpers assisted by many servants. After a moment of reverential silence, the cooks began to cut into the flesh of the giant beast. Removal of the first segment of skin released the most extraordinary aromas. None of the scent of the sea remained. The squid had simply acted as a giant cooking vessel for the other ingredients, whose flavors and textures had commingled to form an indescribably rich and varied fare.

Grain lined the cavity of the squid—first rice and then cracked wheat— each layer being some five feet thick. Nestled in amongst the grains were all the meats which traditionally comprise the second or roast course of a royal banquet. First, the cooks uncovered veal sweetbreads. Next came a series of viands which had been partially cooked by spit-roasting and then finished inside the squid: skylarks with lemon sauce, quails surrounded by eggplants, pigeons stuffed with capers, and rabbits with pine nuts. A variety of larger birds followed. Chicken, geese and ducks, each roasted to a golden brown and accompanied with appropriate fruits, found their way to the now overflowing banquet table. A whole kid goat stuffed with pudding surprised the guests, who applauded appreciatively as it was carried to the table. Next came a haunch of venison covered with a delicious apricot glaze. The course was brought to a close with squares of meat aspic.

By now the Count had drunk enough to have forgotten his manners. He gulped lusty draughts of mead and, reaching, grabbed food off the trays

even before they were brought to his side. Allessandro matched Ammanato glass for glass, but was more subdued in his revelry. He joked with the nobles and complimented the cooks but never for a moment forgot that he was the host.

If anyone at the banquet had been sober and in full control of his faculties, he would have noticed certain odd occurrences at the great table. A noble seated next to the Count grabbed at his food and put it into his mouth with a quick sucking motion. His lady, in a high state of intoxication, found herself irresistibly drawn to squirt dark wine from a bota bag at a handsome young knight across the table. He in turn stared at her with a fixed gaze, almost squid-like in its luminous intensity.

Half the guests had already lost interest in the food and were amusing themselves in a manner which befitted their drunken state. The other half applauded the arrival of the third course. The boiled meats and stews were finished off inside the squid. Bulgur and millet surrounded the boiled meats. First, breast of veal, followed by a goose boiled Lombard style accompanied by sugar and cinnamon. A poached milk-fed calf proved to be the highlight of the third serving. Its flesh was so tender and pink as to almost defy description. Stewed pigeons with mortadella sauce and fricasseed breast of goat completed the course.

By the end of the third serving, all the guests had pushed themselves back from the table to a more recumbent position, some on the couches provided for that purpose, others less elegantly on the floor. Despite the protests of many in the great hall, who claimed that the very sight of the food would make them gag, the fourth course was served to an empty table. If anything, it was of greater quantity than the previous servings: bean and pear tarts, cheeses of every kind, almonds, chestnuts roasted with sugar, and wafers as a final light touch.

As midnight approached, Allessandro rose and invited the Count, nearly asleep in the arms of a maid, to accompany him outside. The two nobles went out arm in arm, leaning against each other the way men always do when they've had a good deal to drink. They walked past the giant oven towards the Duke's shipworks where a warship stood in a state of near completion. The Count commented on the fine craftsmanship, the solid lines and the seaworthy construction of the vessel. As he turned to Allessandro to ask him about the mysterious coverings hanging from the rigging, the Duke, summoning all his strength and conviction, spoke: "I must admit that my inviting you here this evening was not without a special purpose. I could understand that you had no way of really knowing whether I was a commander worthy of your support. I think that I have proved to you that I am an imaginative leader of men. Now I will show you that I am also a man of generosity. Here is my gift to you."

With that, Allessandro's men cut away the shrouds to reveal a sail of a most unusual construction. The pen of the squid had been fashioned into a magnificent mainsail which now shimmered in the moonlight. (The squid's backbone is certainly one of the oddest things in nature. Its shiny transparent substance resembles glass but possesses a flexibility usually found in much softer materials). And so it was that, transfixed by this extraordinary sight, Count Ammanato was finally heard to mutter: "Yes. Yes. How could I deny your greatness? You can have my army and my navy, too."

This tale, you ask, can it be true? Can the squid, primordial creature of the sea, truly be so significant a creature? Reader, I beg your indulgence, for I will now relate an incident which is even more supportive of my squid theory of history. . .

Squid Resources

Kingdom of the Octopus by Frank Lane. This is the definitive account of the life and loves of the squid, replete with documentation of the giant squid and information about various species.

Octopus and Squid by Jacques Cousteau. Cousteau featured squid and octopus in one of his one-hour underwater documentaries on which the book is based. It is profusely illustrated with color photographs and old drawings, features remarkable pictures of squid mating and includes many historical anecdotes.

Twenty Thousand Leagues Under the Sea by Jules Verne. The leading work of squid fiction is most responsible for mythologizing the squid.

"Squids, Jet-Powered Torpedos of the Deep" by Gilbert Voss, *National Geographic,* vol. 131, 1967. Voss is probably the leading American squid expert. His lengthy article includes photographs of an expedition to the shores of Peru, home of a large, powerful species of squid.

Fisheries in Japan: Squid and Cuttlefish, Tokyo, 1978. Here the Japanese have produced an encyclopedic work on squid. There are many magnificent color photographs as well as Japanese recipes. The text is in English. This is an expensive reference work. Anyone wishing to read it would be advised to try an institute of marine science or an aquarium library.

North Atlantic Seafood and *Mediterranean Seafood* by Alan Davidson. Both of these books are systematic presentations of indigenous, edible sea creatures including many varieties of squid. Excellent recipes are included.

Other Aris Books from Addison-Wesley

THE BOOK OF GARLIC by Lloyd J. Harris

Here is the celebrated, legendary work that put garlic on the map in America. From every quarter—gourmets, health enthusiasts, book reviewers—*The Book of Garlic* has been heralded as a very special cookbook experience. Now in a revised and expanded third edition, the book enters the pungent 80s with more of the charm, wit and fascination of the original edition.

"Admirably researched and well written..."   —Craig Claiborne
                                                                                             The New York Times

288 pages, oversized paperback, illustrated, $11.95
ISBN 0-201-11687-1

THE CALIFORNIA SEAFOOD COOKBOOK by Isaac Cronin,
Jay Harlow and Paul Johnson

The California Seafood Cookbook is an encyclopedic guide to seafood cookery. The 150 recipes—with their emphasis on simplicity, fresh ingredients, and ethnic and regional tastes—reflect a unique and innovative approach to seafood cookery.

The book features over 75 superbly illustrated species of fish and shellfish available in California and the Pacific Coast region. At least 50% of these are also found in Gulf or Atlantic waters, making *The California Seafood Cookbook* relevant to seafood lovers everywhere.

288 pages, 7 x 10, illustrated, $13.95 paper, ISBN 0-201-11708-8

Available at your local bookstore. Or address orders or inquiries about these or other Addison-Wesley cookbooks to: Retail Sales Group, Addison-Wesley Publishing Company, Route 128, Reading, MA 01867. Order Department or Customer Service: 1-800-447-2226.